*The eternal word,
the One God, the Free Spirit,
speaks through Gabriele,
as through all the prophets of God—
Abraham, Job, Moses, Elijah, Isaiah,
Jesus of Nazareth,
the Christ of God*

Astral Horror

*Gabriele,
the teaching prophetess and emissary
of God in our time*

Gabriele
Publishing House

"Astral Horror"

3rd Edition September 2022
© Gabriele-Verlag Das Wort GmbH
Max-Braun-Str. 2, 97828 Marktheidenfeld
www.gabriele-verlag.com
www.gabriele-publishing-house.com

Translated from the original German title:
"Horror astral"

The German edition is the work of reference for all
questions regarding the meaning of the content.

All rights reserved

Order No. S340TBEN

Printed by: KlarDruck GmbH, Marktheidenfeld, Germany

ISBN 978-3-96446-355-5

Table of Contents

Astral Horror 9

The astral body—the soul. While incarnated, its energetic aura—called aura or corona— its radiation, is visible as varying nuances of color 10

Every single person and their soul are an immeasurable sending and receiving station 13

This side of life and the beyond are not separate. The individual's free will decides: For or against the cosmic law 17

Everything is energy. Everything that the person thinks, says and does is energy. According to the law of sowing and reaping the person himself bears the responsibility for all transgressions 22

Delusion of freedom through modern means of communication: Undreamed of possibilities via cell phone, computer, Internet 26

Animals do indeed have a soul! 29

A person's works follow him, in his soul 31

Someone who doesn't know himself often remains blind as a soul. Being driven by souls that cannot desist from their desires and vices 35

"Astral Hackers": Earthbound souls "hack" into people's life programs. Example: Foreign programming in computers via viruses and "Trojans" 39

How do earthbound souls proceed in order to bend a person to their will, to influence, besiege and possess him? 44

The causal law weighs and measures precisely. Who bears what blame? 46

The soul that releases energy into a person hangs on the person—like on a drip-feed 53

The disastrous works of the demons. Manipulations on a large scale 56

Interest groups of souls turn certain types of people into suppliers of energy. "An impure spirit goes through arid places ..." 61

Every soul is thoroughly advised and admonished by the spiritual world. "Why does God allow this? Why doesn't He intervene?" 65

How guilt-ridden souls recognize themselves in picture sequences. A turnaround—or a new incarnation? 70

The caste of priests conveyed a distorted image of God 74

The Fall from the Kingdom of God 75

The religious scam of the caste of priests leads to dependency. In the Kingdom of God there is no religion. God is love, freedom and unity 78

God speaks untiringly 81

In the Old Covenant as at present— God speaks to us through His prophetic word. Let us allow ourselves to be embraced by Him! He is the rock 84

*As Jesus, Christ prepared the way home for us.
The Beatitudes from the Sermon on the
Mount of Jesus* 98

*Jesus, the messenger of love from the
heavens. Words of life* 103

"This is the life I want to live" 106

*Respect, treasure and safeguard your life!
After your demise, your soul will live on* 108

*In the innermost part of every soul is the
heart of purity, the incorruptible core of
being. It guarantees to each person the
return to the eternal homeland* 111

*Do not allow the time of grace, the time of
protection, to lapse unused. What makes
a soul earthbound? Every one has his fate
in his own hand* 113

Addiction seeks addicts 118

*A person should be aware
of his divine origin* 120

Astral Horror

Those who don't settle for just words, who don't dismiss words simply with "what's that supposed to mean?!"—but are able to look more deeply, know what the term "Astral Horror" is all about. They think of something repulsive, gruesome, ghastly and horrifying, not only on the physical, material level, but in the spheres of the beyond that is hazy, dubious, intangible. Many a one would think, "We should not deal with such vileness, because whoever enters such a sphere of influence may come into contact with conditions that cause fright, horror and dread."

Among other things, the word "astral" also indicates the astral body of a human being, an immaterial energy that surrounds him. It is his aura, his radiation.

*The astral body—the soul.
While incarnated, its energetic aura—
called aura or corona—its radiation,
is visible as varying nuances of color*

After the demise of the physical body, the astral body withdraws from the dying shell, the person. The astral body is an invisible body that lasts beyond the death of a person; it is also called the soul, or soul-body. The energetic aura, which once surrounded the person and which is now the radiation of the soul-body, is also called the aura or the corona. The aura of a person—which is also the aura, the corona, of the soul—consists of energies of varying nuances of color that revolve in radiation ellipses around the person and, after the individual's days on Earth, around his discarnate soul.

The various nuances of color of the aura of a discarnate soul consist of energetic forces. These are the contents of the feeling, sensing, thinking, speaking and acting of the former person, which readily found expression in the person's radiation shell. Now, they form the corona of the soul. As long as the soul is in the person, the nuances of color change at every moment, according to what and how the person feels, senses, thinks, speaks and acts.

This is what it's like on the Earth, in the coarse-material and in the spheres close to the Earth of the material cosmos and of the finer-material universe. The origin of each and any form of life, however, is the fine-material Kingdom of God. In the eternal Being there are neither human beings nor souls. The radiation of a pure being of the Kingdom of God consists of the divine forces of the law, the seven basic powers of the eternal Being, in which all other basic powers are contained, in turn, as subregions. Thus, seven times seven forces of the law form the divine aura of each spirit being. The pure beings of the Kingdom of God were beheld and created from the eternal universal Spirit, the Father-Mother principle, and are the sons and daughters of God, of the eternal,

All-One Father, who also spiritually personifies the Mother principle.

The corona of a pure being thus moves about in the unencumbered seven basic powers of the eternal Being, which, in turn, contain all the other basic powers in themselves. Also the aura of the human being, likewise of the soul dwelling in him, radiates in seven times seven energetic forces. However, in the human being, these are burdened according to his behavior patterns. The aura, the radiation of the human being, changes at every moment and on a daily basis. Expressed differently: The aura, the corona of the human being is constantly subject to change. This is because the human being unremittingly feels, senses, thinks, speaks and acts. Each one of his stirrings in life is filled with substance. This substance is what constitutes the individual character and the specific value of the human activities. So whatever the human being places into his feelings, sensations, thoughts, words and actions is what marks him—the human being—and his soul. The aura is what mirrors all of this.

*Every single person and their soul
are an immeasurable sending
and receiving station*

Let it be repeated: With the demise of the human being, the astral body, the soul, withdraws from the dying body. It is marked by the inputs of the human being that passed on; for the inputs, the behavior patterns of the former human being, are also recorded in the soul. These specific traits then form the engraving of the soul and its aura, its corona.

The person can, at every moment of a given day, update and position his behavior, that is, give himself a new direction, deciding for what leads to a positive, or else to a negative, way of life. The positive, which the person puts into practice in his thinking and in his way of life, makes him more peaceful, reflective, and his soul brighter. But the negative also marks the person; it clouds his consciousness and darkens his soul. Both, light and dark, are the result of the behavior patterns of the human being, the patterns, which are reflected, in turn, in the nuances of color in his aura. Corresponding repository planets in the material cosmos, as well as in a finer cosmos, absorb these energetic frequencies. Both cosmos are memory sources that are very extensive. Seen as a whole, they could be described in their unity as the "cosmoses." But for a better understanding, let's remain with the denomination of "coarse-material macrocosm" and "finer-material macrocosm."

Every single person and his soul are an immeasurable sending and receiving station. This is also true of a discarnate soul. Via the potential of sending and receiving, which the human being unceasingly stores and updates, he receives each day, at every moment, hints from his memory potential that want to call his attention to heed or rectify this or that, that is, clear it up. This means that, during his existence, it would be his task to put in order those things that do not serve the common good, the unity, the peace and the freedom. There is no interruption in the process of sending and receiving, not even when the astral body, the soul of the human being, is discarnate. As soon as the physical body has died, the same thing takes place: The soul emits its aura, its frequencies, and receives what is active and current in the soul at just that moment. Everything, but really everything, is based on sending and receiving.

The soul of a human being that has passed on thus continues to move in the cycle of sending and receiving. With the sending potential that the human being has transferred to the soul, the latter remains tied to these energy potentials, which formed the engraving of the former human being. They are engraved in his soul.

Like its former human being, the discarnate soul also is stimulated by its sensory perception to recognize and rectify the all-too-human aspects, its offenses—we human beings talk about sins against the cosmic law of love for God and neighbor. According to what is currently active, that is, what is due to be cleared up, the respective pictures develop in the soul body, even whole sequences of pictures from the inputs of its former human being. We could say that these pictures point out to the soul the culpable occurrences through which its human being burdened itself. These pictures thus reveal light and shadow, therefore stimulating the soul to recognize the all-too-human aspects, the sinfulness, to feel remorse and clear them up. Step by step, it should find and walk the path which leads it via the material macrocosm to the corresponding planetary constellation of a purification plane. There, it becomes aware of further active memory inputs, which, in turn, show up in pictures or sequences of pictures. In this way, the reasonable and willing soul is able to bring into lawful order what was waiting to be dealt with.

This side of life and the beyond are not separate. The individual's free will decides: For or against the cosmic law

People who believe in a higher existence, which we call the Creator or God, should be aware that this side of life is not separate from the beyond. The French nuclear physicist, Jean Charon (1920-1998), once spoke about a "universal dialogue of elementary particles," in which he saw what mystics have been describing from time immemorial as the omnipresent, divine love. God is no longer a Creator separate from His creation—He is in it. The beyond and this side of life are not as separate as we think.

In line with this, the physicist Hans Peter Dürr, former head of the Max Planck Institute for Physics in Munich, said the following, "What we call this side of life is basically the dross, matter, that which is tangible. The beyond is everything else, the encompassing reality, the much greater." Seen this way, after death, our consciousness simply goes to where it actually always was.

Let it be repeated: The human being—as well as the discarnate soul—is constantly shown the possibility to rectify the negative, the burdensome. Each day can be for the person a day of recognition and serve to clear up a debt. The human being learns in his thoughts and, at the same time, in his conscience, about those not good aspects that need to be settled. The soul in the beyond experiences similar things in picture sequences that it is made aware of and feels them as suffering or pain, depending on the causes behind them.

To serve our understanding, the following: The soul body is created as a particle structure, as opposed to the physical body, which consists of a cell structure. In its cell structure, as well as in the particle structure of its soul, the human being stores the "pros and cons" of its particular character imprint. So this means that the human being stores the energy potential that is either for the life, which is peace, unity and freedom, or it stores the energies that are against the life, like bindings, a lack of peace, egoism, violence, the all-too-human aspects. Whether human being or soul, the free will for a free decision is inherent in both; either for the cosmic law, which is the cosmic, eternal life, or against the cosmic law, which is given in the will of the ego and has no basis. Based on his free will, the human being is responsible for his own life. The human being, himself, determines whether he burdens his body as well as his soul or liberates them from vileness, from the negative.

If the soul has become detached from the deceased shell, the human being, that is, once it is discarnate, then, little by little, the inputs of its former person become effective. Regarding whatever culpability may exist, the soul can decide freely. Either it follows the path of redemption, which is shown to it via its inputs, or it continues to move in apathy and dullness, just as its human being was: not responsive to higher values, to life in general. If the soul adheres solely to the imaginations of its base desires, passions and drives, then such a soul mostly stays in the in-between realms of the beyond, and tries to siphon energy from those people who have similar weaknesses—depending on what it has as an engraving, as a debt.

Dear reader, perhaps you will be thinking the following: "What help can be given to a person in the entanglement of culpability, in the mill of sending and receiving?" Perhaps you are also wondering if it isn't unjust that the soul carry the debt incurred by the human being. These questions are totally plausible, above all, if the person does not question himself, if he is not aware of why he is a human being and that no energy—whether positive or negative—is ever lost. The soul in us is simply not of this world. It incarnated, that is, it became a human being, to rectify as a human being its negative engravings, the wrongdoings from former incarnations. Before its new incarnation, higher beings showed it what its burdens, its debts, are and what could come toward it, the soul, in the physical garment. So it received explanations and teachings. No soul goes unknowingly into incarnation.

Moreover, instructions in orienting oneself to a balanced way of life were given to humankind by God, who is the life. Through His prophets, God, our eternal Father, gave us countless help for developing good character traits. He gave us a myriad of guidelines for taking the steps that lead to freedom and to peace.

In this connection, let us remember the commandments of God, the unadulterated word of God through the true prophets, and not lastly, the teachings of Jesus of Nazareth. Later, there will be more mention of the words of God through His messengers, the prophets.

Everything is energy. Everything that the person thinks, says and does is energy. According to the law of sowing and reaping, the person himself bears the responsibility for all transgressions

So as human beings, we are called upon to make ourselves aware each day that everything that we think, speak and do is energy. The cells of our body and the particles of our soul absorb the contents of our behavior patterns unceasingly. Everything that has not been expiated, and is thus directed against the cosmic law of peace, of freedom and of unity, has not disappeared—it remains in the soul as an engraving, even when the human shell no longer exists. At some point in time, the causes become effective —either in the human being, or, at the latest, once the person is deceased—in his discarnate soul. In the Bible, which many people consider to be the whole truth, among other things, it is written: *"For nothing is secret that will not be revealed, nor anything hidden that will not be known and come to light." And: "Truly I tell you, until heaven and earth disappear, not the smallest letter, not the least stroke of a pen, will by any means disappear from the Law until everything is accomplished." And: "But I tell you that people will have to give account on the day of judgment for every empty word they have spoken. For by your words you will be acquitted, and by your words you will be condemned."*

Let us view our world and its people from a distance. There is lying, stealing, cheating; celebrations degenerate more and more into eating and drinking orgies; the vices of human beings are often addictions that escalate into excesses, which, when practiced, can hardly be surpassed today. Let's mention just a few of them: Gambling addiction, alcohol addiction, drug addiction, nicotine addiction, eating addiction, computer addiction, quarrelsomeness, abnormal sexual addiction, hunting addiction, vindictiveness, compulsive exploitation of people, which is associated with the craving for power, avarice, rapacity, even up to bloodlust, the compulsive killing of people and animals. The addictions and greed are increasing in unimaginable brutality and violence. Children and adults are abused and raped, for example, without restraint. Wars are advocated and carried out with extreme weapons and a radical use of weapons, through which countless people often die a horrible death. People also don't shy away from killing other people in order to confiscate their belongings, or to gain a position of power at the expense of others by bearing false witness and much more. Since God's mills grind slowly, many a one thinks that all misdeeds go by without consequences or that others are to blame.

The culpability of a deed is not always clear and apparent before the courts; for example, in a verdict, the one is given the right, the other is incriminated and convicted of a wrong; perhaps the secular court even imposes a sentence on him. How often don't we hear in court: "Acquitted for lack of evidence." The one is free; the other is incriminated. The one accused, even pronounced guilty, sees this differently. Many an incriminated one doesn't get over the one-sided court verdict and swears to take revenge. There is no one-sided guilt; even if the other one is acquitted, he, too, bears a certain share of the blame.

Justice is reconciliation. This is why Jesus of Nazareth taught: "*Settle matters quickly with your adversary who is taking you to court. Do it while you are still together on the way, or your adversary may hand you over to the judge, and the judge may hand you over to the officer, and you may be thrown into prison. Truly I tell you, you will not get out until you have paid the last penny.*"

The law of cause and effect measures very precisely and justly each share of the guilt. Thus, an unresolved offense can easily turn a soul into a soul tied to the Earth.

Let it be repeated: All the contents of our feeling, thinking, speaking and acting, that is, the totality of the contents of our behavior, go into the cell structure of our physical body and into the particle structure of our soul.

Delusion of freedom through modern means of communication: Undreamed of possibilities via cell phone, computer, Internet

Our world seems to have grown smaller, among other things, also through the Internet, wireless telephones and other human conveniences of our time.

In a conversation with a computer "geek," the following was described:
Above all, it is the Internet that leads us to believe that the world has become a small village. In fractions of a second we have access to more knowledge and information via the Internet, more so than any of the large libraries of the past ever had to offer. News from all over the world reaches us in seconds. In all languages, all events are only a click of the mouse away, offered in pictures, sound and film. Anyone who wants to comment on this can also do so immediately and,

at the same time, spread it around the globe. From near or far, each person can look at the farthest corner of the Earth from a satellite perspective; he can post information and pictures to this and make it available to all participants of the network. To talk to someone, you don't have to leave your house anymore. Internet platforms make it possible for anyone to talk to countless people from all countries and at the same time. And if you want to see the person you are talking to, you can have a face-to-face conversation directly via your computer with sound and picture, in all the countries of the Earth. Recreational get-togethers, particularly among young people, no longer are organized in the old-fashioned way via telephone, but are made available with pictures, text, sound and film to all those friends that were chosen for this particular activity. And you are not even tied down to the computer at home. On your cell phone, you can be directly reached with all information, regardless of where you are. If you want to know where any one of your friends is at any given moment, you can learn this via the cell phone, because every movement of the owner of a cell phone is stored and is available "online" as needed. Through all these and other technical possibilities, the person thinks that he is "at home" anywhere in the world. Whatever is far away seems to be within reach. And the person feels that the multiple possibilities mean —wrongfully so—freedom.

But the world has not grown smaller, because the repository sources, the cosmoses—the material cosmos and the cosmos beyond matter—have not shrunk. Ever more people live on the Earth; most of them are against one another. Each one, in his insatiable ego-greed, wants to be the greatest. Few think about the fact that they leave in their soul traces of their mania.

Although there are ever more people whose misdeeds gain the upper hand—the repository sources of the cosmoses nevertheless do not have to grow; there is enough room for every soul. The cosmoses have been laid out accordingly, by the One who knows all things, including future developments. And so, let us be aware that every disregard, all addictions and excesses, the brutality, all violence and use of force toward people, animals and nature, toward the whole Earth, is allotted justly to each individual human being and his soul in all detail and is recorded in the repository sources as his respective share of the blame.

Animals do indeed have a soul!

Many people unscrupulously torture animals; they keep them for slaughter in animal ghettos; the animals are often bestially killed in the slaughterhouses; their meat is consumed or they are kept in scientific laboratories for experimental purposes. Human beings act as if animals were lifeless commodities. For example, the hunter slinks through the woods, often hiding in the high seat he built for himself, so that he can underhandedly shoot down the unsuspecting animal, which then—often having been merely wounded—may drag itself along for days on end in fear and pain until it miserably perishes. Or let us think of the farmer who applies his combat agents against the life of the soil, such as, for example, pesticides, fungicides, herbicides, and whatever else can be obtained as a means of extermination. He also spreads animal and human excrements on the topsoil. With all these attacks on nature, the life of the soil contorts in convulsions and then suffocates. The farmer cares little whether the animals destined for slaughter have a miserable existence in unworthy stalls until they are transported to the butcher who then brutally kills them. His religion has determined that animals have no soul; so they are merely an economic factor. The cruel animal experiments are carried out in many places without any stirring of conscience because the religious representatives of certain types of people claim that animals have no soul, that they are nothing more than a commodity to be freely and arbitrarily utilized at will.

Does this coarse society really believe that this and more will remain without consequences? The immoderateness and disregard toward the animal world apparently has no limits. But animals do have a soul, and very much so. Their Creator is God, who breathed the life into them, something we will read more about.

A person's works follow him, in his soul

To repeat, let it be said that human being and soul bear the engraving of all that is antagonistic and which the person inflicts upon his fellowman, but also upon the Earth and the animal and plant worlds. This and more are the works of the individual person, works that follow him. After the demise of the physical body, the works of the person remain in his soul as a corresponding engraving, unless the person recognizes in good time his often bestial, negative behavior, his vices, and remedies them by taking the steps that Jesus of Nazareth showed us. His words state the following: "*Settle matters quickly with your adversary who is taking you to court. Do it while you are still together on the way, or your adversary may hand you over to the judge, and the judge may hand you over to the officer, and you may be thrown into prison. Truly I tell you, you will not get out until you have paid the last penny.*"

It would be good and right if we, each and every person, were to critically and seriously question ourselves each day. For example: "Who am I?" and "Where will I be after my soul disincarnates?" But let us also not be deceived by hypocritical sanctimonies, as we can so often read on the gravestone epitaphs, like, "He, or she, is now with God" or "May he, or she, rest in peace" or "He, or she, has now found peace" or "… is freed from long suffering." And don't believe the well-sounding speeches of the priests or pastors either, who stand at the grave of the deceased with raised voice, giving a theatrical ending using the same old lines such as, "He, God, the Eternal, has now seen fit to take 'so and so' home to Him—earth to earth and dust to dust, may he or she now rest in peace." Or, we hear such things as, "Died in Christ, risen in Christ to eternal bliss," etc., etc. Surely there are more such unctuous words of comfort for the bereaved.

What would the bereaved say if it were said of the deceased, "His works not only follow him, but are engraved in his soul"?—That's how it is! And according to the law of sowing and reaping, according to their causality, they bear fruit.
This has already been passed down, because in Revelations, we can read: "*And I heard a voice from heaven saying, Write this: Blessed are the dead who die in the Lord henceforth. Blessed indeed, says the Spirit, that they may rest from their labor, for their deeds follow them!*"
Let us look more closely at this: What are these deeds, these works, that go with most souls?—In the end, they are all the person's wrongdoings that are still waiting to be cleared up. It simply is the

way it is: After the demise of the person, the soul is what its person used to be!

After the eulogy or funeral oration, we hear for comfort, "I knew this person for a long time." Or, "I knew the deceased for many years."

We should be mindful of the fact that no person, not even a pastor or a priest, can totally figure out another person. The human being is an ambiguous being, who speaks with a forked tongue in many situations. Most people are not even aware of this, because most people don't know themselves. They don't fathom what takes place behind their patterns of behavior. Few make the effort to explore their hidden ways, their ambiguity, by analyzing themselves with the question: Who, actually, am I, really? Most people live in self-deception, that is, irrationally. They vegetate away their days and, as a matter of course, consider themselves to be better than their fellow people.

Someone who doesn't know himself often remains blind as a soul. Being driven by souls that cannot desist from their desires and vices

To the same extent that the person doesn't know himself, his discarnate soul will not get its bearings after the death of his body. The soul will attain more clarity in itself only when a higher being that accompanies the soul can find a way to touch the soul with its advice. The soul will gradually become aware of what is presently active in it as "pro and con," and what lies on the "con" side, the debt, needs to be remedied. But not every soul is willing to accept the help from above, from the beings who are its guardian and teacher. The imprinting that a human being inflicts upon his soul often has far-reaching consequences. A heavily burdened soul, which has engraved on it the human tendency to think that matter alone is the ultimate, will resist every help. Many of these souls have been programmed by their former person and cannot let go of their desires and passions, of their thirst for revenge, of hostility and cruel philosophies of life. Souls that were oriented toward matter by their person don't readily take the steps indicated to them by a cosmic repository planet or a higher being. And yet, this is exactly the path on which the soul could rectify its negativities, its burdens, the path on which it could continue on its spiritual evolution, that is, its further development, in order to truly attain a higher quality of life.

A soul that was programmed with the inclination toward licentiousness is the same as its former person in terms of unfulfilled desires. It is like its person once was. It is bound to sundry human habits, such as prestige, wealth, money, greed, power, as well as licentious desires and much more and will long for the same over and over again.

Let us make ourselves aware of the fact that the human existence is not real. If it were truly reality, the physical body would not have to pass away and then the human being would have everlasting youth. Hans Peter Dürr, the former head of the Max Planck Institute of Physics in Munich said the following, and rightly, "What we call this side of life is basically the dross, matter, that which is tangible." Seen in this way, the human being is satisfied with the dross, which, among other things, is the ego.

Every soul is finer-material and invisible, intangible for the human being. And yet, it is present, for, in terms of energy, this side of life flows into the beyond and vice-versa. If the soul is tied to the world of desires of its former person, then it is open for a new human birth on Earth. In the end, every human birth already bears death. With its incarnation, every soul brings with it into this world what was not rectified in the beyond, as a soul. What was not rectified in the beyond can break open again on this side of life, that is, in a human being.

The life-substance of many people is shaped by virtual ways and means. The person behaves according to this condition, and later, the discarnate soul. As stated, this side of life and the beyond are not separate from one another. Bound to the all-too-human characteristics of their ego-world, there are souls that bend people to their will for their own purposes, people they can reach, people who live in a similar world of thoughts and desires as they do, and who practice those vices that fit their own perverted desires.

Souls which, based on their engravings, cannot let go of this world are also called "earthbound souls." The whereabouts of earthbound souls are the in-between spheres within the material macrocosm, near the Earth.

"Astral Hackers": Earthbound souls "hack" into people's life programs. Example: Foreign programming in computers via viruses and "Trojans"

The souls that we ourselves have programmed and that may be controlled by demons do not utilize anything different than was familiar to their former human being, who, for example, had to do with computer technology. The Demons' State, which fights against God, doesn't develop anything new, but merely reverses the spiritual-divine law for its own base, corrupt purposes.

The spiritual-divine law is: Send and receive and communicate with the All-One, who is God. The adversary reversed it to: Send and receive and communicate with the negative forces.

An example from a conversation with a computer geek can help give insight into many a fatal development. Every computer works on the basis of its programs, which the respective computer owner has programmed into the computer. He works with these programs and saves all the data that he wants to keep. So the decision is left to the owner of the computer what he wants to do with the programs in his computer. He enters into his computer what he thinks is good and right. He saves some of it, particularly what he needs for the long term, and other things, in turn, are deleted because they are no longer important to him. The user of the computer thus moves around in the computer world that has been arranged by him with the programs that he himself chose and enlarged upon, with which he works and from which he develops further uses. This, his individual computer world, is, to an extent, part of his identity.

What happens with a so-called computer virus or a computer Trojan? If an extrinsic computer user wants to utilize the data or operating system to damage it or use the main memory, the RAM, to gain something for himself, then he plants so-called viruses into the computer system. These viruses contain outside programs, which, based on the existing programs, alter the computer to now be utilized for the purposes of the one who intruded on another's computer system, making it serve him. Of course, the owner of the computer will not readily grant entry to the intruder. So how do viruses and Trojans get into the system? In important aspects they proceed quite like the earthbound souls, which seek victims among the human beings in order to appropriate their energy for themselves. Just like the souls, these viruses help themselves to the available programs of the "host," in this case, the computer, in order to slip into the system. Via data, which the computer doesn't recognize as not being its own data at all, because these contain aspects that are the same or like those already stored in the computer, other programs are slipped into the existing operating system. Since these outside programs are basically the same as or like the computer's own programs, the host computer does not recognize them as foreign, but accepts them on the assumption they are its own programs. This is why these outside programs are also called Trojans. Just like the Trojan horse, which was allowed into the besieged city and its soldiers, once there, poured out of the rump of the horse to then conquer the city from within, exactly in this way do the Trojan programs act in the computers. They reveal their real intentions only when they are within the system they want to conquer.

When this goal is reached, then it is possible—depending on the intentions of the outside operator—that the whole programming of the computer can be utilized from without, thus using its storage capacity. Through this, the "host" computer is damaged. Its performance is reduced; it functions deficiently or is even totally damaged and it can even come to a total computer "crash." It is possible that the outside operator, the "hacker," also uses the stored data of the "host" computer to gain, for example, financial advantages. What takes place in the computer world via hackers is basically no different than what the "astral hackers" do with human beings. They virtually use the similarities of the life-programs of the person and his available negative patterns to tune into the "operating system," the human being, that is, to influence and take over him more and more, to occupy him, intending to successively gain the upper hand imperceptibly, and to transform the possessed person in such a way that the contents of the astral hacker's world of programs can be fulfilled. This can then lead to a fatal change in the exploited human being who allows himself to be used. His own habitual programs fulfill and carry him less and less. He becomes more and more a stranger to himself. Such a development can so easily end with the "crash" of this person.

How do earthbound souls proceed in order to bend a person to their will, to influence, besiege and possess him?

Rightfully so, we wonder how virtual astral souls, that is, soul beings, get hold of the corresponding people to bend them to their will and thus, through coinciding programs, experience what agrees with their own world of desires?—The cosmic law of equality states: Like waves of energy always seek out like wavelengths. We also say: Like always attracts like.

The materialistic world of today and its human beings with their virtual thinking and behaving, with their profligacy, their addictions, greed, and manifold excesses and desires offer bound souls a welcome nesting place in their aura and perhaps later, in their bodies. The urge of an earthbound soul is the indispensable desire to again experience everything as it once was for it as a human being, in thoughts and, occasionally, in the deed. Its fascination, what it once lived in thoughts and was partially fulfilled, makes it hope to find a victim, a person of its nature, through whom it can live out unhindered its lusts, its vices, greed and striving for power as a human being, without loss of prestige. The soul is on the prowl. If it comes upon a human being like it, then it tries, as stated, to bend the latter to its will. How does this happen?

Once the earthbound soul has found a human being with the same or like predispositions, the soul emits energy to this person. The intent of the soul is that its victim, the person, desire and do what it has in mind, so that it can influence him and possess him as soon as possible. At first, such souls beguile their victims in a way that is invisible to the person, then they send into his aura kindred feelings: profligate, compulsive behavior, etc., etc. A soul can reach a victim more quickly and easily, in order to influence, besiege and possess him, if the person simply takes each day as it comes without goals of his own, that is, if he submissively carries out what is in accord with the soul's world of desires.

*The causal law weighs and
measures precisely.
Who bears what blame?*

In a conversation with a person who collects information on this, further interesting aspects on the topic "Astral Horror" emerged.

Through the increasing application of technology and industrialization, the Earth, with all of nature, the animals and people, is exposed to the most varying environmental influences to an until now unknown magnitude. No sphere of life is spared today from multiple experiments to manipulate nature and to gain influence over the most varying forms of life via radiation. But let's keep in mind the fact that for every intrusion on the natural, God-given order, the law of sowing and reaping applies—sending and receiving. And each one who sets causes into motion will inevitably have to bear the effects at some point in time. Who has set a cause in motion and to what extent and which effects he has to bear accordingly is precisely weighed and measured in its energy, according to the cosmic justice. If people suffer under global consequences—like, for example, atomic radiation, the destruction of the ozone layer or irradiation from highly technological combat and defense systems—then the one who may make mistakes, or exhibit weaknesses and other things because of these influences does not burden himself. Instead, all those who developed such systems and apply them bear the greatest blame, but also those who endorse them, including the law-makers who create the conditions that make such and similar manipulations possible in the first place.

So if people suffer under such systems, then those affected are not the ones who burden themselves, but those who caused or approved of them. Whatever people do, prompted by manipulation via radiation—whether for reasons of weakness or the influence of their nervous system—does not take effect in the law of sowing and reaping as the guilt of the one who has already been harmed; instead, those who developed and endorsed these systems have to answer for these bad developments.

The same holds true for the waste and immense pollution of the natural resources of the Earth. Through the use of pesticides, fungicides, insecticides, which are spread on the fields in agriculture and kill off the micro-organisms, but also by applying animal excrements like manure and slurry, the groundwater is polluted and the drinking water contaminated. The dirty water has to be treated and partly enriched with chemical substances in order to again be fed into the supply of drinking water for the population. This water that is no longer clean, but burdened with additives, presumably will, in turn, inevitably cause damage. However, the causal law will not attribute the blame to those who drink the water, but to those who contaminated the water through their unlawful actions, thus causing this ill state of affairs.

It is similar with animal breeding. Whoever breeds new animal variations through artificial insemination, for example, turbo cows that produce far more milk than natural; or other animals that gain excessive weight, or male cattle that as breeding bulls are turned into breeding machines—they are the ones who will have to bear the effects of the suffering and misery that was inflicted on the animals. Those who allow such manipulations and have these animals "work" for them, but also those who endorse this, bear the burdens that result from it.

Many a reader may perhaps realize more and more, in view of this explanation, that in the world of thoughts, "astral horror" is real and becoming more and more real.
But let us look further into this. What about the animal testing laboratories? Why are the animals tortured in such a way? Who will have to bear this?—Above all, those who, without conscience, torment them are under the law of sowing and reaping. But this also applies just as well to those who build on what is developed from this, who use it for themselves, that is, who benefit from

it. According to the law of cause and effect, they have to answer for the consequences that arise from this and bear them.

Thus, every single action is minutely, precisely and justly weighed in its energy and allotted accordingly to the people who utilize it.

Let us take a look at an example of the chain of possible entanglements of guilt. Whoever uses the substances gained from animal testing in order to dress himself up beyond a natural measure and gain something for his ego—perhaps to gain a partner for himself—has to bear the effects for his corresponding part of this. And the one disaster brings more, in turn, with it. The person who was enticed into the clutches of the alleged beauty, that is, the partner, will in turn be stimulated to several things, with which he indulges his ego to the point of living out his excessive desires and passions. In this way, it is possible that weaknesses in the said partner can come into effect, which he in turn lives out with other people. In some circumstances, the temptations increase;

the responsiveness to extreme, immoral pursuits escalates. A domineering nature, constant rages, aggressions can be the consequences.

Each one who is in such a chain of guilt has to answer for the fact that suffering is increasing globally and that he also has his part in the original suffering that took place in the animal experiments and the knowledge that was gained from them. Perhaps, for example, further people suffer under the incited and inflated ego aspects of the one who walked into the clutches of the alleged beauty. So there are chain reactions, in which the law of sowing and reaping is perpetuated. And each one who has a part in it will be weighed and measured according to his part—that is, the contents of his feeling, thinking, speaking and doing. The suffering of the animals, the suffering of the plants, the suffering of the people is minutely allotted and the individual will have to bear the effects at some point in time.

Who knows what all will come from the manipulations, be it seeds, cloned animals, genetic manipulations, the addition of substances in baby food and much, much more?—Those who do the research for it, those who try it out, those who utilize it, all of them bear their part. All the consequences that come from it will fall back, on the one hand, on the originator, on the other hand, also on those people who know about it and endorse it, up to those who legislate and the government.

*The soul that releases energy
into a person hangs on the person—
like on a drip-feed*

Every earthbound soul has its specific volume of energy that often is not enough to act upon someone, to influence them, to besiege them or to even possess them. This is why it applies the following: By focusing, it tries to induce people of its caste of mind to direct their thinking in a certain direction, that is to say, to encourage its victims to commit disgraceful deeds. While doing so, it stimulates one or several aspects of radiation in the aura of the person, which correspond to the world of desires of the soul that is doing this. And so, the soul focuses on certain energy pathways in the aura of the person, so that certain aspects are stimulated through his thinking and acting. What was at first perhaps merely latent in the person, now may, with repeated thought, perhaps break through.

For example, the person thinks and thinks with ever more vehemence. In doing so, images come up in him on how it could be and he follows up on his world of desires with actions. In this way, he develops increased energy that automatically is transferred to his aura. The soul that releases energies in the person by focusing hangs on the person as if on a drip-feed. The soul then takes as much energy as it needs from the aura of its victim, to then stimulate another vice in another person, and thus fulfill this vice as well, through the new supplier of energy.

In our world, there are hardly any limits against fulfilling vices, greed, striving for power and much more, even if it is done through a virtual fantasy made possible on the Internet.

Most people are not aware that everything is energy, and that no energy is lost. It is often as if a person were struck blind, because many of us have read or heard about the correlations of energies and, nonetheless, think it does not have anything to do with us.

Let us ask ourselves why shouldn't it concern us, each one of us in particular? Are we beyond the reach of the cosmoses, or don't we question ourselves, our thinking, speaking and doing? Regardless of how a person thinks about this, he is recorded and remains recorded in a detailed way, because the entire content of our sensations, feelings, thoughts, words and actions, that is, all our behavior patterns, is recorded.

All impure patterns of behavior that are not in the superordinate, absolute law, the All-law, move about in the satanic principle of sowing and reaping, or—as we casually say—in the principle of action brings reaction.

With his patterns of behavior, every one of us is unceasingly oriented to sending and receiving. Similar sending potentials of souls can influence the waves of sending and receiving of the individual—depending on their frequency. This takes place when earthbound souls can misuse a certain frequency for their own purpose. This is one of the dangers in our world. The other danger is even more far-reaching, namely, the influence of the demons from the Demons' State, which has settled in the lower spheres of the finer-material cosmos and of the material cosmos, along with other negative forces.

The disastrous works of the demons. Manipulations on a large scale

The Demons' State still clings to the desire to dissolve the creation of God even though by way of His Redeemer-energy, Jesus of Nazareth brought the effective means against the dissolution of all divine forms. From the Absolute, He applied His indissoluble energy force to rescue the divine, eternal creation, all forms of Being, from dissolution.

What does this ominous work of the demons look like? The demons are not content with the energy potential of individual people, as are individual earthbound souls. Demons act upon whole groups of people, on large and smaller assemblages of people. There, where crowds of people come together, they work to incite the masses, to draw them into an aggressive vortex of energy, that is, to bring the people into an even greater frenzy, in order to tap into the energy flows—that is, the concentrated negative energies. These concentrated charges of energy are, in turn, cleverly put to work to bring about further evil in the world, again, through people who serve the dark forces.

Demons are always out to incite groups of people for their purposes, to stir up strife, dissension, until the energy flows, which they then invest in people and groups of people in the world, who, for example, act against God's creation, who crave profit when it has to do with large money transactions or projects involving supraregional resources of the Earth, or to acquire tracts of land or plunder valuable natural resources of the countries or instigate wars, in order to gain power over a country, or bring large sums of money to flow, by which certain people enrich themselves. When it has to do with upholding their tyranny, the demonically influenced power-crazed people do not shy away from subjugating their fellow people, exploiting them, having them raped and killed. Energy is always needed for all these extensive demands of great projects or those power-holders who abuse the Earth and people for their planned, sometimes worldwide, purposes.

At the beginning of the Fall-event, the Eternal, the Creator of all Being, loaned only a certain quantum of energy to the beings who defected from the Kingdom of God. God gave and gives no additional energy for any negative goings-on—whether on a small or large scale—nor for those possessed by wanting to have money and power. This means that every person who craves profit, every earthbound soul or the demons require the energy from people to be able to live out their uncurbed world of desires on the Earth and among the people on a large scale and through individuals.

All negative contents, which, in the end, are a part of the amount of divine energy that was loaned, provide the opportunity and reason to influence us human beings, or even to besiege or possess us. Every impure thought, every behavior that is not a part of the power of All-Creation can be stimulated and reinforced by negative forces via the principle of sending and receiving.

Everything is energy. If thinking, speaking and acting take place within the loaned energy—which we can also call the Fall-energy—then this energy can be influenced. Whoever thinks over and over again about his world of desires, his claims to power and so on and so forth, thus producing negative energy over and over again, comes into the danger zone. There, he is stimulated to continue thinking, speaking and acting in this spirit, so that a soul or demon is able to besiege him. If a certain volume of negative energy has been reached, then it will be siphoned off by the invisible forces. The person has now become a so-called spigot.

The earthbound soul, just like the demons of the Demons' State, needs people in order to rob them of their energy. The individual soul as well as the soul of the demon, which, with like-minded souls siphon off energy on a large scale from crowds of people, all have only their own personal volume of energy that they cannot change on their own unless they earnestly walk the path of purification by recognizing their existing negative inputs in the planetary constellations and remedying all their not-good aspects that were and still are against the law of All-Unity, thus striving toward the Kingdom of God.

Souls cannot take any energy from other souls. On the other hand, people can rob energy from their fellow people, when they have made others dependent on them.

Interest groups of souls turn certain types of people into suppliers of energy. "An impure spirit goes through arid places …"

The influence of earthbound souls on people, so as to fulfill their desires, is varied. In the in-between spheres and in the material cosmos there are also so-called interest groups of souls that make certain types of people their special suppliers of energy by way of influencing them. They want to purposefully utilize these energies on people who, in the temporal, follow similar interests as they once followed, for example, to complete a scientific study that they were unable to complete as a human being, etc.

In the in-between spheres, there are also groups of souls of religious fanatics who belonged to a certain religion when they were human beings and seek to influence those of similar bent, in order to revive their religious convictions, that is, in order to force their religious mania onto others.

The contact with people is always initiated in the same way. As already described, souls programmed by human beings try, by emitting, to stimulate in people that which corresponds to their longing for fulfillment.

If the soul can besiege its victim, the human being, because the latter not only lives out in thought his desires in his virtual world, but also carries them out, by, for example, robbing, plundering, raping, abetting others to murder and much more, then the soul takes possession of its victim. At first, it pushes the soul of the person back and partly enters the physical body to then delight itself with profligate deeds through this person. This was the existence of its former person and it is now the craving of the soul that was programmed by its person. If the possessing soul has reached its goal, then it moves on in order to find another victim that corresponds to its type. If the victim—that person through whom the soul pursued its world of desires—is taken to court, if he has to go to prison or to a rehabilitation center, then the soul often lets go of its victim and looks for a new one—as already stated. Let us think of the so-called gambling dens in some large cities, where addiction is gaining the upper hand to such an extent, that one can talk about automatic "fuel pumps." It is similar with the souls that became addictive souls through such people and then hang on addicts like bunches of grapes.

The words of Jesus can give us manifold information on such processes: *"When an impure spirit comes out of a person, it goes through arid places seeking rest and does not find it. Then it says, "I will return to the house I left." [to the body of a person]. When it arrives, it finds the house unoccupied, swept clean and put in order. Then it goes and takes with it seven other spirits more wicked than itself, and they go in and live there. And the final condition of that person is worse than the first. That is how it will be with this wicked generation."*

What happens in our world that often seems inexplicable also takes place, however invisible to human eyes, in the virtual world of the earth-souls. As stated, the procedure of earthbound souls is always the same. First the aura of the person is sent to, in whose aura the same or similar things are present. Through intense sending, that is, focusing, similar aspects are reinforced and the person's thoughts on vices, desires, passions, greed, deception, lies, theft, murder, rape and the like are stimulated. If the soul is successful, the human victim becomes servile and develops the corresponding images of desires, and then the soul besieges its victim to make it compliant, until the person turns the contents of his thoughts into actions. Through its victim the soul then delights in the debauchery and excesses.

Every soul is thoroughly advised and admonished by the spiritual world. "Why does God allow this? Why doesn't He intervene?"

With these terrible horror occurrences, we should not forget that higher souls are always present, to teach such souls, to help them so that they find their way back to lawful actions and let go of their victims. Whether the soul accepts this help or rejects it is always left up to the soul. Free will holds true for human beings as well as for souls. Every person also has a spiritual guardian being at his side, which, according to free will, admonishes and warns. Whether the person perceives the fine, positive impulses or disregards them, even shrugging them off, is determined by the person himself. In the eternal law of cosmic infinity, free will is a basic, immutable power. The Infinite, whom we people call God, Allah, Jehovah, highest Intelligence or heavenly Father, is always the

One who is the All-Power, Wisdom, Love and Freedom in eternity.

Many readers will think, "This is a horror scenario!"—Correct, it is a horror! It is truly eerie. But who created these conditions, this nightmare that runs rampant on the visible as well as invisible level?

Let us not forget that just as the tree falls, so does it lie. God, the Eternal, gave freedom to the divine beings in the Kingdom of God as well as to human beings. If this is so, then who is to blame? God or the people? It is we, the human beings, through our impure thoughts and desires and with our hatred, envy, hostility, deception, lies, vengeance, murder, rape, including the abuse of the Earth. It is we human beings who have caused and continue to cause immeasurable suffering to the animals and the desecration of nature. Who is it that lives in the intoxication of brutally subduing the Earth, of hoarding money and goods, while placidly watching how his fellow people die of hunger? The existence of many people is a virtual intoxication, thinking this would be the future. Ever more people are stricken with passion, greed, rapacity, compulsive gambling and instability, with being against one another and much more.

It is the human being who is the specter of horror, who, after his physical death, is as a soul the one he was as a human being in the earthly garment. It was his works—and as a soul it is likewise its works.

Many a one could say: "Why does God allow this? Why doesn't He intervene?" We could, however, turn the question around: Why do we human beings allow ourselves to think in such impure ways and abandon ourselves to the violation of moral principles? We can answer this ourselves when the question is: Why doesn't God intervene?—Whom should God grab by the scruff of the neck, that is, seize by a shock of hair and punish for his crimes?

What would you say, for example, if God were to do this to you? Wouldn't you perhaps immediately call out, "What about the other one?! He's much worse than I! This is not fair!" And another would say, "I want my freedom; I want to do or not do as I please."

So, what should God, the Eternal, do with us human beings? God is the absolute justice and freedom, which He bestowed upon all beings, including us human beings, as a divine gift. We ourselves, each one, who always calls for freedom and wants to be free is ultimately responsible himself for what he does and does not do.

The principles of the law apply to each soul in the spheres of purification, but also to each earth-bound soul—that chooses people as victims and that is admonished over and over again to change its ways and follow the path of discernment and purification—these principles are apostrophized with "sowing and reaping" or "cause and effect" or "action brings reaction," and are a part of the Fall-event.

Via the repository planets of the finer-material cosmos and after many indications, the information of guidance is reflected to each soul, that it should set out on the path of discernment and purification. The earthbound soul is given to understand that it should back away from all its lusting, and, like many other souls, follow the path that was prescribed for it and that is shown to it in sequences of pictures. According to this, the soul could rectify step by step what it's former person had burdened it with, through remorse and asking for forgiveness and, if other people were guilty of something toward its former person, by forgiving these people and their souls. Thus, all souls—the tempting ones as well as the tempted ones—receive from the law of life, which is unity and freedom, the same chance for self-recognition and for reorientation.

Many souls, particularly earthbound soul-beings, repress these pictorial impulses. They behave, or react, similarly to a person who is repeatedly prompted via his conscience to look at what the day shows him that is negative, and to ask for forgiveness and to forgive. Many people who feel pangs of conscience shrug this off as a fit of weakness.

What takes place in a discarnate soul also occurs in a similar way in a human being. Yet the person who is oriented to without, to matter, is often of the opinion that only material help and support can be applied as an effective settlement of the deficits. For this reason, he calls for an intervention of human help and the application of power and money—both are not possible among souls.

How guilt-ridden souls recognize themselves in picture sequences. A turnaround—or a new incarnation?

The situation of a soul when parts of its burdens, the sins of its human being, become active, that is, awaken, has been extensively dealt with. How souls may experience these promptings of conscience and picture sequences becomes clear in the following descriptions that may apply as case studies:

In the soul of a former hunter—whether it is in the spheres of purification or as an earthbound soul that claims a human victim—pictures and sequences of pictures develop. In these, it sees how as a human being it ranged through the woods and fields, how the animals were wantonly killed with human brutality, how the animals dragged themselves around for hours or even days until they died. In its own soul-body it sees and experiences as suffering and pain how an animal mother was killed and its young starved to death. The soul sees this and at the same time feels the suffering and the pain of the animals in its own soul-body. Because of the pain, the suffering and the pictures of horror, this soul now desists from possessing people, because it bears and feels in itself the pain of the animals and of the people.

Another soul wanders in its pictures or, invisible to us human beings, it may tramp over the fields of the Earth, with suffocation attacks, similar to those its person once caused to the animals. Or the suffering of the animals, which were cruelly fished from the rivers, lakes and oceans, now causes suffering and pain in the guilty soul. It suffers what its person previously had inflicted upon other beings respectively. All excesses toward people and animals, to the point of greed in wanting to be ever richer, through which others suffered and died of hunger, is experienced in the beyond by the soul of the overly powerful person. Everything, but really everything, that was not paid off by it as a human being, will be experienced and suffered by every soul on its soul-body. Only once person and soul have recognized their terrible deeds, feel deep remorse, once they ask for forgiveness from within and forgive, in turn, does the soul then follow the path that leads to higher forms of life, provided it was forgiven.

After the sequence of pictures, which calls up conditions of suffering and pain in its soul-body, a question comes toward the soul: Does it want to continue to develop in the realms of the souls of the finer-material cosmos, or does it want to incarnate again, when two people, that is, a parent couple with similar programs, offer the soul the possibility to incarnate? How it then continues for the incarnated soul, the person, is determined by the new person, himself.

Life on Earth is extremely dangerous; but no soul is forced to incarnate again. The human being has his own development as a human being in his own hands. Every person is a wayfarer, whose path leads, starting from the Earth, and later as a soul via the spheres of the beyond, to the eternal homeland, to the Kingdom of God—once the consciousness has opened for this. But each person decides himself, how, when, and for how long and where, its soul will linger.

The caste of priests conveyed a distorted image of God

At all times, God, the Eternal, sent divine beings who incarnated as human beings and interpreted God's word, in order to convey His word to the people. Humankind calls the heavenly interpreters the prophets of God. They are the true prophets who do God's will.

The eternal truth of God through His interpreters, through the prophets, was at all times doctored, tailored and falsified by the caste of priests; and what is still in existence as the unadulterated is attributed to the past and tailored and falsified in such a way that what it presented and still presents as God's message corresponded and still corresponds today to the caste's way of thinking and acting as it relates to power.

The caste of priests imposed on God, the Eternal, whatever they wanted. They depicted God to the people as a god of vengeance and an avenger, who condemns His children to death, who imposes on them the eternal punishment of hell, etc., etc. Basically, it was and is the priests, however, who pressed and press the people into a straitjacket with such concepts. God, the Eternal, however, is the love and the freedom. God is just, but not a god of vengeance or an avenger! Whoever looks into this world and does not shy away from looking more closely will recognize who bears the greatest guilt for the state of this world …

The Fall from the Kingdom of God

Often, we read or hear about the Fall from the Kingdom of God. What took place in the Kingdom of God? It was divine beings who rebelled against God's law of love, freedom and unity. They wanted to be God themselves. This phenomenon is surely nothing new to us, particularly when we take a look at the present time and see the machinations of many people, including those of their priests. Almost everyone plays his game with the other one, as though he were God himself, but God, the Eternal, does not play games with His creatures.

However, the many "human gods," who are like the god Baal, the avenger-god, demonstrate the Fall-thought that is: "I am my own best friend. Everything only for me!—I don't care about the other, unless I can use him, that is, abuse him, as I want to." Such a theft of energy is far more widespread on the Earth than we would think. Apparently, we human beings are heading toward the lowest point, toward self-adulation. According to the law of cause and effect, as a soul we will be just as we were as human beings. In the beyond, we will then continue with our self-delusion in a similar way.

But let us briefly return to the estrangement from God's love, freedom and unity. God, the Eternal, gave the renegade beings, His children, a substantial amount of positive, divine energy to take with them as a loan. Many of us know that everything is energy and that no energy is ever lost. Fall-cosmoses formed by way of this loan from God—we call the one the material cosmos and the other, which exists above the material cosmos, the finer-material cosmos. The finer-material cosmos is the place of residence of the souls where further cosmic soul-realms open up. These are called Order, Will, Wisdom, Earnestness. On the path to the Kingdom of God, Kindness, Love and Gentleness are added. The stars and planets of both cosmoses consist of countless repository planets, which justly record the "for and against" of the person and his soul, that is, they register and update it at every moment according to the patterns of behavior of the person.

The religious scam of the caste of priests leads to dependency. In the Kingdom of God there is no religion. God is love, freedom and unity

The bad state of our world with its people is, on the one hand, to be attributed to the indifference of the people and, on the other hand, to their dependency on religions and their priests. Priests of all types founded external religions. By putting the fear of God into people, a practice that has found expression in countless cults, rites and dogmas, people are tied into the religious scam with the statement that it is solely the guild of priests that has the truth. At all times, the caste of priests tried and tries to put the noose of dependency around the neck of its believers, provided with the engraving that says: "You have to! Whoever does not do what corresponds to our doctrine and whoever does not belong to our religion is eternally damned."

Is such a thing written in God's law of love for God and neighbor, of freedom and unity? Such binding ecclesiastical regulations of the law have nothing to do with God, who is the love, freedom and unity.

In the Kingdom of God there is no religion, however it may call itself; there are no ceremonies, no rites, cults and traditions. God, the Eternal, is the All-law. He, the All-One, is the Creator in His creation. He is the life in nature, in every animal, but also in the soul of each person.

God is the Spirit of freedom. His power is the I Am—God in us, God in His creation, indivisibly and eternally present in "I Am the I Am."

Nor did God, the Eternal, send any divine beings, who, as human beings, He consecrated as priests! Priests proselytize for their religion and bind the people to people. Jesus of Nazareth, the Christ of God, calls upon the people to follow Him, that is, Jesus, the Christ. He rejected the whole guild of priests with the following words: "*But you are not to be called rabbi, for you have one teacher and you are all brethren.*"

Jesus of Nazareth said the following—and it is also passed on in the Bible of the churches and should give us something to think about: "*Do not think that I have come to abolish the Law or the Prophets; I have not come to abolish them but to fulfill them.*" He did not say: I have come to fulfill the word of the priests! May the one who has ears to hear, hear! And yet, the majority of the people listened and listens to the caste of self-consecrated priests and pastors. If what the caste of priests taught to the people, and in which so many church believers believe and are bound to, were the truth, then today the Earth would be in much better shape: It would be a flourishing planet. Then the people would respect and appreciate God, the Creator of life, by fulfilling His will. God, the Creator, loves His creatures. He is present in soul and person, in the animal and in nature; in all the cosmoses, God, the law of love, unity and freedom, is effective.

As a rule, the priests and those faithful to their religion know only what corresponds to the law "divide, bind and rule." With this divisive and dominating principle, they have led the Earth to the brink of collapse and turned their believers into their subjects.

God speaks untiringly

No person can claim that God never spoke or that God no longer speaks today. God, the Creator of life, speaks untiringly through His creation. In the word, He spoke and speaks to us human beings. Jesus came to fulfill the law and the word of God through the prophets of God. What, for example, did God teach through Moses, Isaiah and through the greatest prophet, Jesus of Nazareth, who became the Redeemer of all souls and people on the cross at Golgotha? Through Moses, God, the Eternal, gave the people excerpts from His eternal law of love, freedom and unity. Through Moses, God spoke "you shall"—the caste of priests teaches its followers, those faithful to its religion, "you must." In the Ten Commandments of God, lies freedom, but also the responsibility of each one of us. Freedom also obligates! We human beings are free beings, however, we have freely taken on the responsibility for our life.

Who does not know the Ten Commandments of God, or who hasn't ever heard about them? What we read or hear from the Ten Commandments of God is freedom and not the pressure that was and is forced onto many members of religions by the laws of the church, in which is always said, "you must!" The statement "you must!" contains, at the same time, the pronouncement of damnation in the following sense: Whoever does not follow this or that is eternally damned.
And, to receive an answer to the question "why?" in terms of the many horror scenarios given above, we can inform ourselves not only in the Ten Commandments of God, but also in the word of God given through Isaiah and, above all, in the teachings of Jesus of Nazareth.

The Ten Commandments of God:

The first commandment: "*I am the LORD your God. You shall have no other gods before me.*"

The second commandment: "*You shall not misuse the name of the LORD your God.*"

The third commandment: "*Observe the Sabbath day by keeping it holy.*"

The fourth commandment: "*Honor your father and your mother.*"

The fifth commandment: "*You shall not kill.*"

The sixth commandment: "*You shall not commit adultery.*"

The seventh commandment: "*You shall not steal.*"

The eighth commandment: "*You shall not give false testimony against your neighbor.*"

The ninth commandment: "*You shall not covet your neighbor's wife.*"

The tenth commandment: "*You shall not covet your neighbor's goods or possessions.*"

The Ten Commandments give us guidance on a life that is in the will of God. With them, we can tell to what extent our all-too-human patterns of behavior may not be in the will of God. Anyone who wants can compare the Ten Commandments to the topic of "Astral Horror."

In the Old Covenant as at present—God speaks to us through His prophetic word. Let us allow ourselves to be embraced by Him! He is the rock

Let us now turn to the words of God through Isaiah. Let us compare them to the body of thought of today, the egocentric desires, the maltreatment and torture of the animals, the wanton killing of animals and the consumption of animal meat, and not lastly, the cruel animal experiments!

By comparing people's doings today to the statements of God through Isaiah, we will understand much better the subject of "Astral Horror." The word of God through His prophets is attributed to those times by today's caste of priests. But yesterday is also today.

God spoke, for example, through Isaiah:
"The multitude of your sacrifices—what are they to me? says the LORD. I have more than enough of burnt offerings, of rams and the fat of fattened animals; I have no pleasure in the blood of bulls and lambs and goats. ... Stop bringing meaningless offerings! Your incense is detestable to me. ... I cannot bear your evil assemblies. ... When you spread out your hands in prayer, I will hide my eyes from you; even if you offer many prayers, I will not listen. Your hands are full of blood; wash and make yourselves clean. Take your evil deeds out of my sight! Stop doing wrong, learn to do right! Seek justice, encourage the oppressed. Defend the cause of the fatherless, plead the case of the widow. "
And what is it like today, during our time, in our society? The one who can grasp it, may he grasp it: Astral Horror!

Further excerpts from the word of God through the prophet Isaiah:

"Woe to those who rise early in the morning to run after their drinks, who stay up late at night … but they have no regard for the deeds of the LORD, no respect for the work of his hands. … Therefore the grave enlarges its appetite and opens wide its mouth; into it will descend their nobles and masses with all their brawlers and revelers.

Woe to those who call evil good and good evil, who put darkness for light and light for darkness, who put bitter for sweet and sweet for bitter. Woe to those who are wise in their own eyes and clever in their own sight."

Comparing the actions and doings of today's humankind to the word of God through the prophet Isaiah, highlights ever more clearly the subject "Astral Horror."

Through the prophet Isaiah, God further proclaimed to the people:

"The earth dries up and withers, the world languishes and withers … The earth is defiled by its

people; they have disobeyed the laws, violated the statutes and broken the everlasting covenant. … Its people must bear their guilt. Therefore earth's inhabitants are burned up, and very few are left. … The floodgates of the heavens are opened, the foundations of the earth shake. The earth is broken up, the earth is split asunder, the earth is violently shaken. The earth reels like a drunkard, it sways like a hut in the wind; [in terms of the people:] *so heavy upon it is the guilt of its rebellion that it falls, never to rise again."*

When we compare the word of God through Isaiah with the topic "Astral Horror," every question that says, "Why does God allow this?" is answered.

Continuing with the word of God through the prophet Isaiah:

"And these [here, the priests and false prophets are meant] *also stagger from wine and reel from beer: Priests and prophets stagger from beer and are befuddled with wine; … Who is it he is trying to teach? To whom is he explaining his message?*

For it is: Do this, do that, a rule for this, a rule for that; a little here, a little there.
Therefore hear the word of the LORD, you scoffers who rule this people in Jerusalem. You boast: We have entered into a covenant with death, with the realm of the dead we have made an agreement. When an overwhelming scourge sweeps by, it cannot touch us, for we have made a lie our refuge and falsehood our hiding place."

The task that is given to us in relation to the topic "Astral Horror" is the following: compare, compare and again compare, and reflect about yourself in your "for and against."

And God continues to speak through His prophet Isaiah to us people:
"I will make justice the measuring line and righteousness the plumb line; hail will sweep away your refuge, the lie, and water will overflow your hiding place. Your covenant with death will be annulled; your agreement with the realm of the dead will not stand. When the overwhelming scourge sweeps by, you will be beaten down by it. As often as it comes

it will carry you away; morning after morning, by day and by night, it will sweep through. … Now stop your mocking, or your chains will become heavier; the Lord, the LORD Almighty, has told me of the destruction decreed against the whole land."

May the one who has ears to hear, hear! And for the one who has a conscience, may it be a lesson. Yesterday is today, and tomorrow, "Astral Horror" will be even clearer. God's word through the prophet Isaiah:
"Go now, write it on a tablet for them, inscribe it on a scroll, that for the days to come it may be an everlasting witness. For these are rebellious people, deceitful children, children unwilling to listen to the LORD's instruction. They say to the seers, See no more visions!, and to the prophets: Give us no more visions of what is right! Tell us pleasant things, prophesy illusions."
May the one who has ears to hear, hear! The one who looks deep into the words, may he decide— for or against. God is the freedom. The one who binds, speaks untruth.

The word of God through His prophet Isaiah, to us human beings:

"Your teachers will be hidden no more; with your own eyes you will see them. Whether you turn to the right or to the left, your ears will hear a voice behind you, saying: This is the way; walk in it. Then you will desecrate your idols overlaid with silver and your images covered with gold; you will throw them away like a menstrual cloth and say to them: Away with you! He will also send you rain for the seed you sow in the ground, and the food that comes from the land will be rich and plentiful."

God, the Eternal, untiringly extends His helping hand to His children, regardless of whether they are discarnate beings, that is, souls, or people. God's word is valid, yesterday and today.

God spoke through the prophet Isaiah:
"If you do away with the yoke of oppression, with the pointing finger and malicious talk, and if you spend yourselves in behalf of the hungry and satisfy the needs of the oppressed, then your light will rise

in the darkness, and your night will become like the noonday."

And further, we can read:
"But your iniquities have separated you from your God; your sins have hidden his face from you, so that he will not hear. For your hands are stained with blood, your fingers with guilt. Your lips have spoken falsely, and your tongue mutters wicked things. No one calls for justice; no one pleads their case with integrity. They rely on empty arguments, they utter lies; they conceive trouble and give birth to evil. They hatch the eggs of vipers and spin a spider's web. Whoever eats their eggs will die, and when one is broken, an adder is hatched. … Their deeds are evil deeds, and acts of violence are in their hands. Their feet rush into sin; they are swift to shed innocent blood. They pursue evil schemes; acts of violence mark their ways. The way of peace they do not know; there is no justice in their paths. They have turned them into crooked roads; no one who walks along them will know peace. … But whoever sacrifices a bull is like one who kills

a human being, and whoever offers a lamb is like one who breaks a dog's neck; whoever makes a grain offering is like one who presents pig's blood, and whoever burns memorial incense is like one who worships an idol."

What God, the Eternal, spoke through Isaiah, is valid, also for today:
"I revealed myself to those who did not ask for me; I was found by those who did not seek me. To a nation that did not call on my name, I said, "Here am I, here am I." All day long I have held out my hands to an obstinate people, who walk in ways not good, pursuing their own imaginations—a people who continually provoke me to my very face, offering sacrifices in gardens and burning incense on altars of brick; who sit among the graves and spend their nights keeping secret vigil; who eat the flesh of pigs, and whose pots hold broth of impure meat; who say, "Keep away; do not come near me."

When we people of today hear yesterday's word of God through Isaiah, then we very gradually become aware of the fact that God is the same. The Eternal, God, is unchangeable, yesterday, today and tomorrow. Whoever reads and has learned to understand, whoever knows how to analyze will become more and more familiar with the topic, "Astral Horror."

God, the Eternal, our eternal, heavenly Father, spoke at all times, and does so today, as well, into the conscience of the people. But he who will not hear will feel, at some point in time.

The Eternal continued to speak through Isaiah: *"I am the first and I am the last; apart from me there is no God. Who then is like me? Let them proclaim it. Let them declare and lay out before me what has happened … Is there any God besides me? No, there is no other Rock; I know not one."* May the one who has ears to hear, hear. The one who knows how to analyze looks deeper into the statement of the Word of God through Isaiah which reads: *"No, there is no other Rock; I know not one."*

"This is what the LORD says: I am the LORD, who has made all things, who alone stretched out the heavens, who spread out the earth by myself, who foils the signs of false prophets and makes fools of diviners, who overthrows the learning of the wise and turns it into nonsense, who carries out the words of his servants and fulfills the predictions of his messengers.

You heavens above, rain down my righteousness; let the clouds shower it down. Let the earth open wide, let salvation spring up, let righteousness flourish with it; I, the LORD, have created it."

The Eternal announced through Isaiah the New Era, the incipient Kingdom of Peace of Jesus Christ; for His Son, our Redeemer, the Christ of God, comes in the Spirit:

"The desert and the parched land will be glad; the wilderness will rejoice and blossom. Like the crocus, it will burst into bloom; it will rejoice greatly and shout for joy. … Water will gush forth in the wilderness and streams in the desert. The burning sand will become a pool, the thirsty ground bub-

bling springs. In the haunts where jackals once lay, grass and reeds and papyrus will grow. And a highway will be there; it will be called the Way of Holiness; it will be for those who walk on that Way. The unclean will not journey on it; wicked fools will not go about on it. No lion will be there, nor any ravenous beast; they will not be found there. But only the redeemed will walk there. …
I will make rivers flow on barren heights, and springs within the valleys. I will turn the desert into pools of water, and the parched ground into springs. I will put in the desert the cedar and the acacia, the myrtle and the olive. I will set junipers in the wasteland, the fir and the cypress together, so that people may see and know, may consider and understand, that the hand of the LORD has done this."

Through Isaiah, God gave witness that He loves all animals, that He is the Creator of all beings, of all of nature. God speaks into the Kingdom of Peace, for His Son, the Christ of God, will appear in the Spirit.

"The wolf will live with the lamb, the leopard will lie down with the goat, the calf and the lion and the yearling together; and a little child will lead them. The cow will feed with the bear, their young will lie down together, and the lion will eat straw like the ox. Infants will play near the hole of the cobra; young children will put their hands into the viper's nest. They will neither harm nor destroy on all my holy mountain, for the earth will be filled with the knowledge of the LORD as the waters cover the sea. …

See, I will create new heavens and a new earth. They will build houses and dwell in them; they will plant vineyards and eat their fruit. My chosen ones will long enjoy the work of their hands. Before they call I will answer; while they are still speaking I will hear."

The helpful hand of the Eternal always endures. Thus, He, the All-Wise, spoke through Isaiah:
"But my salvation will last forever, my righteousness will never fail. Hear me, you who know what is right, you people who have taken my instruction

to heart: Do not fear the reproach of mere mortals or be terrified by their insults. ... But my righteousness will last forever, my salvation through all generations.

. . . Give ear and come to me; listen, that you may live. I will make an everlasting covenant with you, my faithful love promised to David. ...
When you cry out for help, let your collection of idols save you! The wind will carry all of them off, a mere breath will blow them away. But whoever takes refuge in me will inherit the land and possess my holy mountain."

Words of life! May the one who can grasp it, grasp it; may the one who wants to leave it, leave it.

As Jesus, Christ prepared the way home for us. The Beatitudes from the Sermon on the Mount of Jesus

Dear readers, the subject "Astral Horror" shows only in fragments what many souls experience, but also endure, after discarding their physical body. We human beings are nothing other than wayfarers on the way to peace, on the way to the eternal homeland, to our eternal dwelling places of which Jesus spoke when He said: *"In My Father's house are many mansions; if it were not so, would I have told you that I go to prepare a place for you?"*

All people, all wayfarers on the way home into the eternal Father's house, are more or less sinners. But on our journey, we should daily reflect on the Ten Commandments of God through Moses and on the many indications given by God, the Eternal, through His prophet Isaiah and other divine prophets.

Moreover, 2000 years ago the Son of God came to us, Jesus of Nazareth. He taught us the Golden Rule that says: *"Do to others as you would have them do to you!"* And said in an even more understandable way for us people, it is: *"What you do not want another to do to you, do not do to anyone else!"*

On our way into the Father's house, as human being and as soul, we should become blessed beings step by step, who are more and more one with the eternal Father, who is in heaven. Every human being is free in his thinking and living. This is why no human being can beatify a soul. Jesus of Nazareth did not teach such a thing. But every soul that strives heavenward will be a blessed being at some point in time, because it will again be one with God, its Father and ours. It is particularly the Beatitudes, which Jesus of Nazareth taught us in the Sermon on the Mount, that give witness to the fact that we ourselves can attain salvation by fulfilling the eternal law of God, which is love, peace and unity, the love for God and neighbor.

"Blessed are the poor in spirit, for theirs is the kingdom of heaven.

Blessed are those who mourn, for they will be comforted.

Blessed are the meek, for they will inherit the earth.

Blessed are those who hunger and thirst for righteousness, for they will be filled.

Blessed are the merciful, for they will be shown mercy.

Blessed are the pure in heart, for they will see God.

Blessed are the peacemakers, for they will be called children of God.

Blessed are those who are persecuted because of righteousness, for theirs is the kingdom of heaven.

Blessed are you when people insult you, persecute you and falsely say all kinds of evil against you because of me. Rejoice and be glad, because great is your reward in heaven, for in the same way they persecuted the prophets who were before you."

Each one of us who wants to figure out his life on Earth in its very depths can take all his attitudes and behavior and compare them to the Beatitudes. In this way, each one of us will gradually find his way to himself, in order to recognize himself in his own feelings, sensations, thoughts, words and actions.

The calls of woe that Jesus, the Christ, taught us from the law of life can also be a help to us in order to recognize ourselves in the very depths of our attitudes and behavior. At some point, each one of us has a little bit of time to take what God spoke through the prophets and through the greatest prophet, Jesus of Nazareth, who became our Redeemer, and compare it to his existence on Earth.

Jesus of Nazareth taught us to follow Him, the Christ of God. He did not instruct us to follow priests. His word is clear and explicit. He taught us:

"But you are not to be called 'rabbi,' for you have only one teacher and you are all brethren."

However, Jesus also taught us the following:
"Settle matters quickly with your adversary who is taking you to court. Do it while you are still together on the way, or your adversary may hand you over to the judge, and the judge may hand you over to the officer, and you may be thrown into prison. Truly I tell you, you will not get out until you have paid the last penny."

To compare the words of Jesus of Nazareth with the subject "Astral Horror" provides an answer to many things.

Jesus, the messenger of love from the heavens. Words of life

Jesus of Nazareth taught us the love of enemy. He said: "*You have heard that it was said, Love your neighbor and hate your enemy. But I tell you, love your enemies, do good to those who hate you.*"
When we also compare this statement of Jesus of Nazareth to our topic "Astral Horror," then we understand more and more why it is as it is: partly hidden here on Earth and evident to the souls in the beyond.

Jesus of Nazareth was the messenger of love from the heavens. He taught us people the law of heaven, the law of the true life. Jesus taught:
"*For if you love those who love you, what reward have you? Do not even the tax collectors do the same? And if you greet your brethren only, what do you do more than others? Do not even the tax collectors do so?*"

Jesus of Nazareth showed us the way to perfection. He taught us the following:

"And if you desire something which causes another pain and sorrow, tear it out of your heart. Only in this way will you attain peace. For it is better to endure sorrow than to inflict it on those who are weaker than you. Be therefore perfect, as your Father in heaven is perfect."

Words of life from Jesus of Nazareth: *"Be therefore perfect, as your Father in heaven is perfect."*

Jesus taught us the direct prayer, the "Lord's Prayer." With simple and plain words, He praised His, our, heavenly Father in prayer, whom we should worship in the very basis of our soul, without intercessors, regardless of whether these have been beatified or canonized by human beings.

In the Revelation of John, the following is written: *"Who shall not fear You, O Lord, and glorify Your name? For You alone are holy."*

And in Matthew we find the following words of Jesus:

"Do not call anyone on earth your father; for One is your Father, he who is in heaven."

In prayer, it is always about God, our Father. We know from God, the Eternal, and from Jesus, the Christ, that every person is the temple of God and that God dwells in us.

The one who compares the words of God through the two prophets, Moses and Isaiah, and through the greatest prophet, Jesus of Nazareth, who became our Redeemer, and compares them with his personal life, with his respective intentions, his feelings, thoughts and words, but also in terms of the doings in this world, will understand better and better the topic "Astral Horror."

Dear readers, what we human beings impose upon our soul and encumber it with is not only sad, but rather scandalous. Many people know that no energy is ever lost. To where shall the energy of each one of us go?

"This is the life I want to live"

The life on Earth is indeed dangerous, but as a soul, we chose it ourselves. We incarnated freely as a human being, in order to rectify as a human being what perhaps burdens our soul from previous incarnations.

The following poem illustrates this statement:

Before I came into this earthly life,
I was shown how I would live it.
There were troubles; there was grief,
There was misery and the burden of suffering.
There was the vice that was to seize me,
There was the delusion that captivated me.
There was the quick rage, in which I rampaged,
There was hatred, arrogance, pride and shame.

But there were also the joys of those days
Filled with light and beautiful dreams,
Where neither lamentation nor vexation exist,
And everywhere the fount of gifts flows free.

Where love gives the bliss of letting go
To the one still bound in the garment of earth.
Where the one who escaped human pain
Thinks high thoughts as though a chosen one.

I was shown the bad and the good,
I was shown the fullness of my failings,
I was shown the wounds that ran with blood,
I was shown the angels' helping deed.
And as I so beheld my life to come,
I heard a being ask the question:
If I dare to live this life,
For the hour of decision was at hand.

So once more I weighed all the bad.
"This is the life I want to live,"
My answer resounded strong and decided,
And I quietly took on my new fate.
And so, I was born into this world,
So it was as I entered a new life.
I don't lament when often I'm not glad,
For I affirmed it when not yet born.

(Author unknown, Attributed to Hermann Hesse)

*Respect, treasure
and safeguard your life!
After your demise, your soul will live on …*

When, as human beings, we pass on, the energy we have sent out is not nullified. Everything we do and refrain from doing is energy, which is recorded as a sequence of pictures like a film, which according to the cosmic law, stimulates the person—and after it discards its body, the soul—to rectify whatever is pending from our energy-inputs.

Unfortunately, our soul can be described as the "holding tank" of our negative energies. The human being is responsible for every "pro and con." We human beings, as well as our soul-body, store everything.

If you, dear fellow people, think about what is written here, which is only a very brief sketch of what all takes place in the astral spheres, then perhaps you will feel compassion for your soul, which, via your conscience, refuses to accept without further ado your all-too-human excesses of every type and means.

If a person has killed off his conscience to such an extent that he no longer feels, or perceives, its impulses, then the soul can no longer defend itself. It stores whatever the person inputs into it. During our daily life, let us think about the fact that the soul stores the entire content of our feeling, thinking, speaking and acting, all our excesses, everything that is against the Will of God, against the cosmic law, and furthermore, all this is stored in corresponding repository planets of the cosmoses.

From person to person, I ask you to respect, treasure and safeguard your life! Life has no boundaries. After your demise, your soul will live on. Where? This is determined by each one of us, ourselves, because just as the tree falls, so will it lie.

Many readers who concern themselves with the topic "Astral Horror" will use such words as "atrocious" or "I don't want to have anything to do with this," when referring to the earthbound souls that carry out their nefarious deeds on people, or even describe them as "diabolical." Who are these obsessed souls that influence, besiege, possess people, or play their wicked games on them? And where do they come from? They come from the human bodies that have passed on. The human being is today what tomorrow the soul will be after discarding its body. No one knows whether he will still be a human being tomorrow, because no person knows when his last hour will strike.

In the innermost part of every soul is the heart of purity, the incorruptible core of being. It guarantees to each person the return to the eternal homeland

In the very basis, in the innermost part of every soul, including the earthbound soul, is the heart of purity that is God. We also call the heart of purity the incorruptible core of being of the soul. The incorruptible core of being of the soul is untouchable, that is, it cannot be burdened, because it is in direct communication with the infinitely eternal Being, the Kingdom of God, and is ultimately also protected by the Redeemer-deed of Christ. Through the incorruptible and protected core of being in it, every soul is ensured that when it has purified, that is, cleansed, itself, it will return as a divine being to the eternal homeland, to its primordial roots.

The Christ of God, the Redeemer of all souls and people, gives the guarantee for this, for He is the way, the truth and the life, and no one comes into the Kingdom of God except through the guarantor, the Christ of God.

Many a conscientious reader comes to realize more and more that earthbound souls are not earthbound by chance. They are always people who have burdened the indwelling soul to such an extent that it cannot get away from the Earth and from people, and that it remains addicted because the human being was addicted, whereby addiction can be something quite complex or many-layered. It can be an addiction to the ego, to dominance, to jealousy, to sexuality, to drinking and eating, to the Internet and much more. A part of this is also the addiction to passion that is often nursed in thoughts, for example, the addiction to murder or to torment or the addiction to delighting oneself in the suffering of others, etc., etc.

*Do not allow the time of grace,
the time of protection, to lapse unused.
What makes a soul earthbound?
Every one has his fate in his own hand*

Every person is granted a so-called time of grace, we can also call it a "time of protection." Every person is protected for a certain time by the positive power in him from the core of being and by his guardian being.

During this so-called time of grace or protection, it is pointed out to the person again and again that he should keep the inner values, of which Jesus gave us an understanding in the following, "Do to others as you would have them do to you." Or said in a different way, "What you do not want others to do to you, do not do to another." Still another person will be made aware in a different way of the Ten Commandments of God. Or we will receive a writing with the content of the Sermon on the Mount of Jesus. Or suddenly the word "Christian" preoccupies us.

In our thoughts, we feel the urge to read about what Jesus of Nazareth taught.

There are many, very many indications, which are the guidance from within, from the very basis of our soul, from the core of being in us, or directly from our guardian being, which inputs many, many things into us, because it accompanies us. But many a one dismisses everything with the words: "That was once!" or: "I don't want to know anything about it!" or: "I don't want to live like that!" or: "I don't want to think that way!" or even: "All that should be left to the old people!" or even: "It's a weakness to think or to live in that way. I will live as I please!" …

A so-called time of grace or protection can last for several years, with some people, even many years, depending on when the time of protection starts. But at some point, this span of time inevitably comes to an end. The positive energies withdraw. The person is now challenged as to how he wants to live, how he wants to be, because the positive power is the divine in the very basis of each soul. It is the free Spirit of life, which does not spoon-feed or decide for the human being and soul. And our guardian being, our invisible companion, orients itself according to God's will.

And then the question proves to be the following: What has the person accepted or only conditionally accepted during this time of grace, or protection, or did he completely and utterly altogether reject the many indications and help? Each person determines this himself. The human being is what he makes of himself. How he thinks and lives becomes his character; that is his nature. Everything, but really everything, that the person thinks and speaks on a daily basis, what he does, what addictions he acquires, how he treats his fellow people, what drives him and what he carries out from this, how often, how intensely and for how long—all this is nothing other than energy, which the person transfers to his soul during the course of his days on Earth, of his life on Earth. At the end of his life on Earth, the soul is then what its person was, perhaps burdened with avarice, addictions, fornication, a programming via the Internet, etc.,

etc.—that reaches the protective cloak, the core of being, the primordial heart of the soul.

It is totally up to the person himself, whether he makes his soul earthbound by tying it to the thorn of his flesh.

To this extent, the question is answered of who the earthbound soul is and where it comes from.

So today, to whom befits the attributes of "atrocious, impossible, appalling" or even "diabolical"? Who is it that, with all possible negativity, enslaves his soul, which should be following the path to the eternal homeland? Is it a rare type of monster that rampages with viciousness, that one describes as "atrocious, impossible," "something we shouldn't deal with" or even "diabolical"?—It is none other than the person himself, for he is the one who decides about his soul. Just as the tree falls, that is how it will lie. And just as the person calls into the canyon, that is how it will echo back. The attitude and behavior of the human being on this side of life is the echo from the beyond, the call of his soul.

Therefore, any one of us who believes in the existence of a soul that incarnated into a human being as an ethereal being, as a fine-material form, in order to clear up as a human being on this side of life what it had caused and not rectified in a previous incarnation, should thoroughly think over his life on Earth. He should question himself, what evil really lies behind his attitudes and behavior on this side of life, in order to rectify it in time, before the tree falls.

As stated, no person knows when the last hour will strike for him as a human being. Perhaps already tomorrow, that is, after our physical demise, we will be who we were as human beings today. Today we are called a "human being," tomorrow, a "soul." Tomorrow, as a soul, we may know ourselves just as little as we know ourselves today as a human being. Most people simply live through the day, nursing their ego and perhaps their programs of addiction, whereby in today's time, there are ever more opportunities for addiction, and they don't even know—or don't want to know—what is in effect behind their external, driven behavior. They are not aware of who they really are. They do not give an account of themselves. They do not take full responsibility for what they do or do not do. Perhaps as a soul tomorrow, they will not know themselves either. For the one who does not question his life, his thinking, speaking and doing, is a stranger to himself.

Addiction seeks addicts

To be numbed with egoism and other programs of addiction can last a long time. The time until a soul lets go of its programs of addiction may be controlled by various forms of seduction. The influences are very many. There are different forms of latching onto human beings by the egocentricity and addictions of the soul. Today, the person is addicted, tomorrow the soul may be raving mad when in a soul that was made addictive by the human being, the program of addiction strongly breaks out and wants to provide for itself an avenue of expression. What is it like for us human beings? If an addiction cannot immediately be satisfied, then quite often the addicted one goes wild. Similar things can be seen with souls. If a soul that was made addictive by a person cannot live out its program of addiction that was forced onto it by the person, if the soul cannot apply it because no human being is accessible to it, then it becomes raving mad. We can say that the addiction always seeks out an addict; the accumulated backlog of frustration then takes on the form of raving madness.

Perhaps these words can help many a one to think about himself. The request to you, to all of us is: Pay attention, may we all pay attention to the content of everything that we utter and what we want and do. We transfer everything, but really everything, to our soul. A request to us all: Turn back, let us all turn back! Let us turn away from everything that is impure, from everything that besets us and that is against every kind of higher ethics and morals! Do not allow yourself, let us not allow ourselves, to be tempted and seduced! Let us take good care of our body and of our soul; for, as mentioned, just as we are today as a human being, we could perhaps be as a soul already tomorrow. For none of us human beings knows when his last hour will be.

A person should be aware of his divine origin

We human beings have become estranged to nature in many different ways. And yet, in nature, the eternal Spirit, God, can be even more directly effective. Every animal, every plant, every stone lets itself be borne and led by the divine ray of power, which arranges and regulates the course of its life.

For example, many migrating birds build their nests in the northern climes and raise their young there, until all of them fly south—often thousands of kilometers away. In the following year, they return and move into the nests they left behind. After such a long time and such great distances, the migrating birds precisely find the way back to their home. They know their place of destination. And what about us human beings? Are we aware of where we come from? Most people know nothing about their eternal homeland. Even the knowledge of the way home has been lost to us, although God, our heavenly Father, has shown us the way through His prophets again and again, and at that, even today, during our time. And nevertheless, each one will have to follow this path at some point in time. Let us make use of the days of grace that are given to us!

Edifying wishes that are in the will of God go with you through your life on Earth. May your path be the way into the Father's house! We human beings—each one of us—decide at every moment about ourselves in terms of the direction our path will take. This also applies to the soul after our physical demise. We hold it in our hands: Either the path leads into scenarios of horror or into light-filled planes, where the soul is shown its next steps into true blessedness, into the true, the eternal freedom, to Him, God, our heavenly Father, and to our brothers and sisters in the Kingdom of God. It is only then that we are eternally at home, in the dwelling places that Jesus, the Christ, our Redeemer, showed us.

Good wishes go with you,
Gabriele

The Path of Forgetting
The Microcosm
In the Macrocosm

The truth about each one of us lies in the stars. The heavenly bodies know each one of us through and through … How can we understand this?

In this book we are led into the lawful principles of life in a very unique way, and this opens up in us new dimensions of our existence. Universal correlations between the microcosm and the macrocosm are explained in such a way that they convey the lawful processes that lie behind all life.

Gabriele explains how everything that we as human beings feel, think, speak and do, is not only unceasingly recorded in the microcosm "human," but is also in constant communication with further memory sources in the coarse-material macrocosm and, beyond that, in a finer-material macrocosm.

Whoever not only reads the contents of this book, but thinks about it and relates it to everything that they encounter at every moment, will find that new knowledge opens up to them, the far-reaching significance of which is of unspeakable value for shaping their life.

124 pp., SB, Order No. S 348en, ISBN: 978-3-96446-355-5

We will be happy to send you
Our current catalog of books, CDs and DVDs,
as well as the free excerpts on many different topics:

Gabriele Publishing House—The Word
P.O. Box 2221, Deering, NH 03244, USA
Toll-Free Order No.: +1-844-576-0937

Read Also:

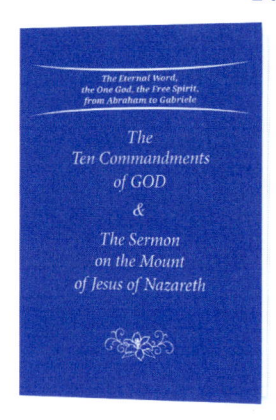

The Ten Commandments of GOD & The Sermon on the Mount of Jesus of Nazareth

Everything that we need to live in peace with one another and in unity with nature and the animals has been given to us for thousands of years: They are the universal values contained in the Ten Commandments of God and in the Sermon on the Mount of Jesus of Nazareth.

However, the Sermon on the Mount was dismissed as utopian and the Ten Commandments were simply ignored or changed as desired—yet these fundamental principles of the law have nothing to do with religions or churches, but rather are excerpts from the eternal law of the love for God and neighbor, and are valid for all people, regardless of faith, culture or nationality—as a free offer from the Kingdom of God. All people are free to apply them or not, but one thing is clear: They are not utopian but can be lived and lead us to inner peace and freedom, drawing us closer to God in us.

222 pp., SB, Order No. S182TBEN, ISBN: 978-3-96446-264-0